MW00773449

HEART

BOOKS BY MEENA ALEXANDER

POETRY

Stone Roots

House of a Thousand Doors: Poems and Prose Pieces

The Storm: A Poem in Five Parts (chapbook)

Night-Scene, the Garden (chapbook)

River and Bridge: Poems

The Shock of Arrival: Reflections on Postcolonial
Experience (poems and essays)

Illiterate Heart

PROSE

Women in Romanticism: Mary Wollstonecraft,
Dorothy Wordsworth, and Mary Shelley

Nampally Road: A Novel

Fault Lines: A Memoir

Manhattan Music: A Novel

TRIQUARTERLY BOOKS

NORTHWESTERN UNIVERSITY PRESS

EVANSTON, ILLINOIS

ILLITERATE

HEART

M E E N A

ALEXANDER

TriQuarterly Books
Northwestern University Press
Evanston, Illinois 60208-4210

Copyright © 2002 by Meena Alexander. Published 2002
by TriQuarterly Books/Northwestern University Press.
All rights reserved.

Printed in the United States of America

10 9 8 7 6 5 4 3 2 1

ISBN 0-8101-5117-0 (cloth)
ISBN 0-8101-5118-9 (paper)

Library of Congress Cataloging-in-Publication Data

Alexander, Meena, 1951–
    Illiterate heart / Meena Alexander.
        p. cm.
    ISBN 0-8101-5117-0 (cloth : alk. paper) – ISBN 0-8101-5118-9
(paper : alk. paper)
    1. India–Poetry. 2. Immigrants–Poetry. 3. East Indian
Americans–Poetry. I. Title.
PR9499.3.A46 I45 2002
811'.54–dc21

                                                2002000269

The paper used in this publication meets the minimum
requirements of the American National Standard for
Information Sciences–Permanence of Paper for Printed
Library Materials, ANSI Z39.48-1984.

FOR MY FATHER

Who can show
the workings of a heart
by tearing it in two?

– Hala, *Gāthāsaptaśatī*

CONTENTS

PROVENANCE

The bowl on the ledge has a gold mark
pointed like a palm.

I leave the bowl empty,
its pallor pleases.

Plain glass marked with a sign
of no lasting consequence.

I lead you into the page.
With you I enter a space where verbs

have little extension, where syntax smolders.
I hear you murmur:

What consciousness takes
will not survive itself.

I repeat this as if knowledge
were its own provenance, as if the sun

had never risen on intricate ruins,
Mohenjo Daro of the mind: cool passageways.

A grown woman might stoop to enter,
gazing at walls stuck with palm prints,

and on damp ground, pitchers of gold
holding clear water.

SHE HEARS A GOLD FLUTE

I am walking over snow
no, not toward you
but toward that place
where the hills are blue.

Under her coat
the woman wears a sari,
under her boots
her skin is dark.

Come give me your hand,
I am going over stones
stumbling to a place
I never thought I'd know.

She hears a tin drum,
she hears a gold flute
at the door to a house,
a small house of stones.

instruments of
heritage? or culture
Shock

Come give me your hand,
my skin is so dark,
my heart is so hot
on this great hill of bones.

7

HEAT WAVE

The body has marks on her,
body marks.
In the discrete music of the furnaces
leaves lilt and pour.

Pride goes before a fall,
Don't be like me.

My father weighs ninety pounds,
there is sweat in his mouth,
his feet are on fire.
He is dying like this.

I am flushed clean of all ambition,
the bruises on my thighs are cornelian.
Who will set a seal on this?

He is upright on the damp bed.
Through a barred window
I see him for what may be the last time.

There is no fear in love.
Fear is torment.
I learnt that once.

8

I touch sharp snakeskins
blown across tarmac,
cracked tablets of earth,

leaves on a bush
ten thousand miles
from my father
scorched into gold.

PORT SUDAN

I hear my father's voice on the phone.
He wants me to come from America to see him
he does not want to die and be put in the earth,

my sweet father: who held me high above the waters
of the Red Sea when I was five,
who saw a white ship docking at Port Sudan

and came sprinting for me
through a crowd of laborers
forced to raise bales of cotton to their heads.

Someone cried *Kef Halek!*
My skirt spun in the wind
and Arabic came into my mouth

and rested alongside
all my other languages.
Now I know the truth of my tongue

starts where translations perish.
Where voices cease
and I face the image of the Pharaoh,

the one who murmured at the hour of his death,
throat turned toward the restless waters:
If I forget Upper Egypt,

cut off my right hand.
Here lies memory.
The same man loved his daughter so

he knew she needed knowledge
of the imprints of earth:
glyphs cut in granite,

inscriptions on rough cloth,
underwater moorings,
and the black sun of death.

morning: death

ELEGY FOR MY FATHER

I
adressing dead person

Father, when you died, your bones
were brittle, fit to burn. — *Hinduism, yet she is Christian*
They stretched you on a teakwood bench.
Light etched your cheekbones,
stoked your eyes, your thumbs
were pale as love–apple fruit. — *metaphor*

The sun when it splashed
into the Arabian Sea
made candles gleam in rows
all along your ribcage.
Kneeling at your throat
I heard a fever bird call.

poet: reflecting the physical of dead body of father

II

One night returning late,
I was a loudmouthed teenager then,
I caught you at the dining table,
fists clenched,
forward bent in darkness.

12

Do you love me? I asked,
needing God knows why to know.
Some things need not be said,
you replied.
I heard the sea roar in your bones.
Of course, you added softly,
under your breath.

Smoke poured from your cigarette.
I learnt to read a kindness
in your clenched fists,
the nicotine scents misting
mother's vase of iron colored roses.

III

You were the age I am now,
a man for all climates,
hot streams, monsoon rivers, the indigo sea.
When they cut India in two
they made you choose.

You were in Karachi,
a young man trained in meteorology,
that science of precise instability.

Learning to measure
the pour of wind,
tor of sunlight,
warm shards of gravity.

Twenty-six years old, jaunty in peaked cap,
starched shirt, gray flannels,

13

[handwritten annotations in margins:]
Father-daughter moment
anger
admits love for daughter "under breath" ques'n
kindness behind outward veil of toughness
image: father smoking
weather; never quite accurte yet precise

the best the local tailor could provide.
I imagine you like young Gandhi,
eyes fixed to a mirror,

adjusting collar and tie,
wanting French lessons, dancing lessons,
surrendering to the equipoise of knife
and fork.

Then came the barbed wires of Partition,
the misery of packed trains,
crude bloodletting.

And ever after England,
with her rationed eggs,
garden parties at Buckingham Palace
for visiting students,
Bible classes in Keswick.

In those hills
you feel God so close,
you whispered, sitting up in bed.
In your ribs I heard
the thud–thud–thud
of an animal heart

that means to keep pace
with the terrible light of God.

IV

When they laid you on the bench
our kinfolk knelt on mats,
sang of grace that slips through black water
to a country that has no shore.

14

However hard you row, Jehovah
is a sun without source.
He will flood you with light.

At your open grave
three priests beckoned me.
The oldest child, I had to cover your eyes.

I bent over your body,
drew out pale muslin,
folded it over your face.

If this is the end of life,
the three priests sang,
what use are *gnanam*,
dhanam, *kavya*?
Princes and potentates
have come to this
crawling on all fours.

After I covered your eyes
a warm rain
fell over teak and mango trees.

We turned eastward
away from the open grave,
fronting resurrection.

v

Father, it is a year since you died.
The past makes sparks and fragments
pour in my eyes.

15

I am in another country,
east of ours, an island
at the rim of the South China Sea.

The land makes a rampart,
a broken glittering geography.
Who stands behind me?

Memory believes.
Can knowing remember?
Someone with white hair beckons me.

She sings an air I do not know.
She kneels under a rain tree,
flings grains of sticky rice into the sea

as the sun soars into that darkness
Plotinus sought
when he mused on the soul,

its very shape a flaming mystery.
There, there, she sings.
Your lips, throat, eyes,

where are they now?
What light will etch us close?
There, there, she sings

pointing to a cloud streaked with pink,
a leaping indigo wave,
Almav avide, avide, avide!

In memory of my father, Kannadical George Alexander, 1921–98

16

[Handwritten annotations:]
trying to console poet
poet upset over fathers death
memorable physical characteristics
rhet. questions
+ repetition

READING RUMI AS THE PHONE RINGS

I

Mother's old sewing machine starts its crick–crack.
She sits in a room fixing the tear in my child's shirt,
red fabric melting into metal teeth.

Some tear, others sew, mused Rumi.
After father died mother barely left that room,
her head bent to the sewing machine.

The door to that room is teak
cut with the pattern of roses and flames.
One night in America, when my belly was huge as a furnace,

when I couldn't tell the door out of the dark,
I saw the phone line spark.
It was father: Why not call your son Abraham?

It's David's father's name,
progenitor to the people of the Bible.
Before my child was born, before my skin tore

in a way no stitching could heal,
I dreamt him with Abraham's dreadlocks,
lips sweetened with honey from desert hives.

17

He would feed off locusts and rosehips,
sip from springs in the city of angels.
When father lay dying on his wooden bed,

the California dates I brought, plump dark flesh,
were what he loved most.
Mother stewed them in well water,

mushed them in her fingers, set the warm stuff
on his tongue. In the dry places of his heart
father heard the whisper of desert roses.

II

The phone on my table is squat and black,
it flickers in the dark.
The voice is hoarse, quivering a little.

He proclaims his name
at the very start—
Shams ul Din, in search of beloved Rumi,

thrust out of Konya
by jealous hands, forced to hitch
a camel ride, then switch to a dusty lorry.

He stands outside a hospital ward in Old Delhi.
I hear the clatter of bicycles, metal milk cans,
cross talk in Hindi, Urdu, Farsi.

My blood test is positive, for sure I'll fall,
Shams mutters, then cries out Rumi's name
in such a way I know

it's hurt from having been cast out:
you're dead meat!
I will never let you into my heart again.

I listen to him pound the tin walls of a shack.
His fist is bloodied, black.
The way of love

is not a subtle argument,
Rumi sang. *The door*
there is devastation.

III

We're crouched before a household god,
mother and I. It creaks, lacking machine oil.
Its clatter marks a figuration for the dead,

the cloth of her life seamed with blood,
married fifty-one years
and his breath snuffed out.

She picks out a finished shirt, smoky, damp.
One day my skin will be like hers,
crinkled with the scent of burnt stars.

Mother shuts her eyes, feeds in her own sari.
I tug her back, not meaning to raise my voice so.
She's confused at seeing father, shirt ripped in all that heat,

ribs raised, smoke in his mouth.
For the sake of Abraham his friend,
he makes the fire glow.

He blows
the furnaces of Nimrod
into eglantines and wild roses.

IV

In a desert of roots I see bits of bone, fiery scars.
Roses bloody with thirst.
Those I have loved turn their faces from me.

I see someone squat in the shadow of a stone,
on his lean shoulders, wings of bone.
He raises up the *Mathnavi* of Rumi in both his hands.

Above his head, crushed cartilage, molten cells,
bits of thread, snapped needles, the wheel and crank
of a sewing machine, beloved bodies

strung into bits, black nostril and knee,
flushed cheek, torn tongue emblazoning
the blue where Shams ul Din has fled for love of Rumi.

My strange familiar stands erect.
His hair is filled with sparks from the wheat fields
of Cincinnati where he was born.

He stretches out his hands to me.
Touching him I dissolve into love's elements:
ash, semen, musk of mother's milk,

alcohol from the hospital wards
of Delhi, crude machine oil,
attar of wild roses.

20

Free Verse
Maymeter on
Assonace on
sound.

MUSE

phoenix is
made but
unmade when it
dies so does
time/poetry

Goddess
phoenix
& muse
inspire in her our
language.

I was young when you came to me.
Each thing rings its turn,
you sang in my ear, a slip of a thing
dressed like a convent girl –
white socks, shoes,
dark blue pinafore, white blouse.

A pencil box in hand – *girl, book, tree* –
those were the words you gave me.
Girl was *penne*, hair drawn back,
gleaming on the scalp,
the self in a mirror in a rosewood room,
the sky at monsoon time, pearl slits,

in cloud cover, a jagged music pours:
gash of sense, raw covenant
clasped still in a gold-bound book,
pusthakam pages parted,
ink rubbed with mist,
a bird might have dreamt its shadow there

spreading fire in a tree *maram*.
You murmured the word, sliding it on your tongue,
trying to get how a girl could turn

into a molten thing and not burn.
Centuries later worn out from travel
I rest under a tree.

You come to me,
a bird shedding gold feathers,
each one a quill scraping my tympanum.
You set a book to my ribs.
Night after night I unclasp it
at the mirror's edge,

alphabets flicker and soar.
Write in the light
of all the languages
you know the earth contains,
you murmur in my ear.
This is pure transport.

transcending to heaven?

CHORIC MEDITATION

[handwritten top right: Where the wild things are is where the poetry begins]

I know where I saw the pasteboard wall:
[handwritten: ok] by the steps of Grand Central Station,
WILD THINGS painted on it, matted fur
and pointed claws, a river sketched in indigo
with tall trees of the jungli sort *[handwritten: pun of word psychologist]*
to hide the mess of pipes, a stairwell exposed and singed.

As I brush past the wall
I hear a voice: *Cara, write your poem well.*
The hard poem about the self
when there is nothing else quite like it,
a tiny "i" cleft from its shadow,
hardly breathing, form's terror.

And the upcoming storm –
I heard about it on the radio –
riffles the leaves of the maple
by the station steps,
flusters the seller of hotdogs,
the lone buyer of newspapers.
[handwritten: activity on voices]
Shall I stand up and sing,
make choric meditation in a time of difficulty?
We live in a raw territory.

25

Bristling things we cannot name take hold.
The fig tree by the river of my childhood
bears no fruit, its leaves are scratched with steel.

In the shade, someone whose face is turned away
is crying out loud.
I am your soul, she sings, her arms open wide,
your dark body alive: press through the wall
into the humming station, swim in the black river
as if you were a girl again and find me.

Finding
herself?

rediscover part of
herself.

FRAGMENTS

I start to write fragments
as much to myself as to another.

(Who lives in my mind?
Can the mind hold its hope?)

I want to write:
The trees are bursting into bloom.

I felt it, though it did not come
in that particular way, the sentence endstopped.

Could sense come in feverish script
finicky with rhyme, sharp as a wave?

Or was that the wrong way around?
The hold of things was perpetually askew,

hard as I tried to figure it through:
a branch surprisingly stout

thrust out of the main trunk
level with my ankle,

the slash in it bright gentian,
cupped in a bracelet of dew.

MAP

I am writing a simple set of directions,
a map to no place in particular:
At the head of the stairs turn right,
when you find yourself at the end of the landing
swing open the bare door – bare meaning
scraped free of vermilion lacquer.

In the white room at the window's edge,
polished free of grime, is a mirror.
Where all that is falls
pictureless, abyssal.
What turns and echoes?
What burns the inner ear?

A spot on the mattress
propped up on the floor,
darkness by the basin,
a snip of hair
bronze in a sudden
bend of light

and on the upturned bucket in the corner
a bottle of antimony,
a silver stick at its rim

beckoning her eyes,
the pupils brilliant indigo,
edgy, inscrutable.

What the mirror never finds
is vanishing.
Somehow you hear a voice cry
in lost vernacular:
Where is God these days?
You answer with tilting hands, a child again,

and turn to face a wave of light
at the mirror's edge.
You know it can pitch houses over,
shred staircases, landings, floors,
into splinters of molten wood:
eternal evanescence.

HOUSE

You set it up: an armature of bamboo,
doors wide open, threshold in sparks.

What does it mean to summon up ancestors –
make them responsible,

make them speak to us in the way a body
lined with flame might, had it voice?

Best perhaps at the water's edge
on a mound lit at the rim with flares.

Muse of memory, maker of sense,
barely lit by mirror or lens,

your house is a package of reeds
flickering in a lake at twilight.

What would it cost to etch
your supernal architecture?

What pitch of gravity?
What squaring of loss?

CIVIL STRIFE

The ink was very old,
palm leaf brushed with the bruise of indigo.
In ancient silk I heard a bird sing
the body's emptiness, a sari swirling on a twigtip.

In the mirror I saw a girl turn into a tree,
her fingers blossoming freckled petals,
greedy hands tore at her,
she fell handless footless into a ditch of dirty water.

Soon there was an altercation
in the frame of things.
I could not tell when the threshold stopped,
where barbed wire would work its bounty.

A child's toe starred crimson,
bullets in guava bark,
civil strife
crowding the rivers.

I had to tell myself that birdsong
in a partitioned land
is birdsong still.
And if moving were not music

of its own accord
I might have stuck forever
at the mirror's rim,
seeing a child see a naked thing

split from a misty tree,
her self as other parting company.
But the monsoon broke,
the river coursed unpredictable.

Black water drew me home.
In my own country
I saw cotton, linen, silk,
blown into threads,

the bridge of belonging
shattered,
cherished flesh
burst into shards of thingness,

a summer surplus,
a bloodiness.
I felt all this fall out
of any possible business of the ordinary.

Yet what was the ordinary but this?
In the tale the girl–tree is recognized,
her scent inexorable draws her lover on.
Moving metamorphosis.

Yet what could this mean to me?
I sought out the philosophers, read Nagarjuna:
If fire is lit in water
who can extinguish it?

In trains and planes,
whose quicksilver speed kept me alive,
I murmured after Heraclitus: One summer day
at the water's edge *I set out in search of my self.*

For Ngũgĩ wa Thiong'o

INDIGO

Already it's summer
a scrap of silk floats

by a vat of indigo.
Ai, that monsoon wind!

Each shadow has its muse.
No one can read your handwriting.

I almost wanted it that way
then came memory –

knee back, tiny toe,
thighbone, brushed in blood.

Each shadow makes a ruse.
My script hovers

at the edge of the legible.
O muse of migrancy,

black rose
of the southern shore!

Already it's summer,
clouds float in silk,

I search for my self
in the map of indigo.

MIRROR OF EARTH

Drawing on ground is not what it seems:
the wind turns you around
quite close to where the twigs splatter.
One caught in my bicycle wheel
and cracked with a loud *treep*.
I could not sleep that night

musing on what you had called
the delirium of history.
Were you quoting someone?
What on earth did you mean?
But even while listening to you
I was trying to figure out what the moths were doing.

One big creature opened its brown wings
and hung on the screen door.
It was as wide as the mandala I made on the dry earth,
a wafer-thin thing outspread
to catch the tunnel of light through the trees.
I worked in what I hoped was imitation

of the Tibetan monk I saw decades ago in Delhi.
He carried palmfuls of sand,
allowing the grains to brush the air,

a bright mortality.
Us, in a mirror of earth,
glimpsed in rare transport,

the self turned outside in
approaching where there is no turning back.
So I gathered soil
and trickled it over my thumbs
and let my bare feet catch the shadow of the twigtips.
When you came to see the moths at play,

only the big one, speckled and soft, was left.
It hung on the door
an edgy susurrus
and you thought you could hush me so quiet.
As I stood watching your hands
I was whispering: That one is called Death's Head.

GLYPHS

I went by Cascadilla Gorge and slid down to water,
a thin sheet rose over my anklebones,
the rising and wetting of it polished my brain.

Sandstone, ripplestone, slate,
the ice-age inscriptions are on me,
tumult of glyphs, zone of grace

where I need not fend for myself anymore.
I see the double-jointed seed of the sycamore
afloat in summer air.

One fell on your bare thigh
as you stooped at my threshold
centuries ago

watching as I cut the letters of our names
in hard soil with a stick.
The water parts my bones,

it makes a sanctuary
and I do not know how I learnt to spell
out my days, or where I must go.

VALLEY

Be grateful for the rain when it falls.
The valley is full of bits –
plane wings, glider strings, parachute straps,
all the unreal equipage washed clean.
And erstwhile passengers shedding kin.

Why am I here? I cannot tell.
They left me here so long ago
so I could flourish as a green bouquet
by a red–tiled house
streaming with rain.

I have no name,
I think you know. You murmur:
The ocean is the hardest thing.
And I: How did we get here
surrounded by hills rough as waves?

I touch your shoes, sturdy leather,
knotted with rain, dangling free,
your shoulder blades bronze
as a parachute string, picked clean by sun,
drawn sharp by earthly gravity.

MAN IN A RED SHIRT

Quick! Are there other lives?
— *Rimbaud*

I

We are poor people,
a people without history.

She saw his shirt,
red cotton, open at the throat,

hair on his chest
taut as the wind blew.

She could not tell
which people he meant,

his shirt open in that way,
his flesh hard under coarse cloth.

II

If she were to write a poem
it would start like this:

[handwritten: red signifies union in India]

[handwritten: Wind blows = sex?]

43

A woman stood at the edge of a terrace,
saw white letters someone scrawled

FROM THURSDAY ON TILL NEVER
THIS JOURNEY IS A NARRATIVE OF LOSS.

Beyond the terrace
is a river few boats cross.

III

Call out the phoenix, let it shake
its wings, soar over water.

What burns is loss. History comes
without cost, in dreams alone.

Our poverty is in the nerves,
the stubble of migrancy, tied up with hope.

Stacked in a wooden boat,
the sails lie flat.

IV

She hears his words:
Let us be one people.

Man in a red shirt,
why move me so?

Touching you,
will I know how the wind blows?

44

TRANSLATED LIVES

The past we make presumes us
as pure invention might, our being here compels it:
an eye cries out for an eye, a throat for a throat.

We muse on Rimbaud's mouth caked with soil,
his Parisian whites stiffening:
Quick! Are there other lives?

Who shall fit her self for translation?
Letter for letter, line for line,
eyes flashing at squat gulls

on this mid–Atlantic shore
with sailboats rudderless,
a horizon scrawled in indigo.

What water here, or air?
A terrible heat comes on,
birds scurry

swallowing their own shadows,
lovers couple on hard rock
groping for the sea's edge.

Neon mirages mock
the realm Columbus sought.
In Times Square selling the National Debt

electronic numbers triple on the light strip
and where the digits run – pure ciphers – 000
mark heaven's haven.

Into that nothingness, a poverty of flesh,
track tanpura and oudh,
the torn ligaments of a goat's throat,

still bloodied, strummed against sand.
As boats set sail through our migrant worlds,
as faxes splutter their texts

into the crumpled spaces in our skin
and the academies bow low: white shirts, threadbare elbows
scraped into arcane incandescence,

shall we touch each other stiffened with sense,
bodies set as if in Egyptian perspective,
full frontal, necks craned to the glint of the horizon?

Will a nervous knowledge
a millennial sense be kindled?
Must the past we make consume us?

GOLD HORIZON

I

She waited where the river ran
that summer as the floods began –
stones sinking,
fireflies murmuring in paddy fields,

herons on stumps of tree
the axe planted
where little else would work
and everywhere the mess of water.

So you have entered a new world.
Her voice was low, growling even.
There was nothing humble in her voice.

Sometimes the dead behave in that know–all way,
ploughing the ruts of disaster,
their unease part of our very pith,
what the axe discovers marrow and meat to us.

So what's it like there? she asked.

I replied: As the Hudson pours
the river wall clings with glinting stones.

47

Yet what's so bright
makes for odd imaginings.

Sometimes I feel as if a metal bowl
had split, dented by blows from a woman's fist
and bits of spelling lessons,
shards of script
struck from a past locked into privacy

– this is the immigrant's fury, no,
who understands my speech,
further what is my speech? –
dropped, pounding as rice grains might.

You think that bowl's your head
your words a crypt.
Look at your feet!
How can you stand addressing me?

I heard her laughing bitterly.
What's with you? I shot back.
What's with the dead, sheer jealousy?

Her fingers waved a whitened scrap,
paper or cloth I could not tell.

She held it out to me:
Take! Eat!

I saw the sari that bound her
dropping free,
feet cut at the ankles,
severed from her calves,
slicked with red earth.

Water poured in short streams
over her mutilated parts.

She stood, shored by a single elbow,
against a mango branch.

      II

Place names splinter
on my tongue and flee:

Allahabad, Tiruvella, Kozhencheri,
Khartoum, Nottingham, New Delhi,
Hyderabad, New York,
the piecework of sanity –
stitching them into a single
coruscating geography
(a long drawn breath
in an infant's dream might work)
ruined by black water in a paddy field.

We wrestle on wet ground,
she and I, living and dead,
stripped to our skins,
naked, shining free in
the gold of a torn horizon.

Our thrashing is not nice.
Her ankle stumps shove against my eyes.

Words bolt, syllables rasp –
an altered script,
theater of memory
I could never have wished.

Breathless I search for a scene,
a mile of city blocks,
iron bridges scraping short hills,
asphalt pierced with neon plots,
the rage of sense:

bodegas in the barrio,
Billy's topless bar,
Vineeta's Video Store crammed with cartons
of Nutan and Madhuri

– *"Kya, kya hum kon hai? Idher hum kon hai"*
"Namal ivide ara? Ivide namal ara?" –

The mixed–up speech of newness,
flashing as a kite might,
pale paper on a mango branch.

III

She waited where the river ran
that summer as the floods began.

Is this mere repetition,
or the warm sprawl of time,
inscribed in limestone?

Who can cry back into a first world
a barefoot child on a mud forking path,
fields gold with monsoon water,
haunt of the snail and dragonfly?

What makes the narrative whole?

Beneath my cheek I feel
her belly's bowl
thick with blood,
the woman who waits for me.

Are these her lips or mine?
Whose tongue is this
melting to the quick of migrancy?

I touch raw bones,
the skull's precise asymmetry.

As rivers north and rivers south
soar into tongues of mist
parting all our ribs

I hear voices of children
whisper from red hills:

An angel, you have caught an angel!

AN HONEST SENTENCE

I cannot see my mother.
Yet I see Agamemnon striding up the hill,
his fists turned to butter,
his small girl led quietly to the mast.

How can I bring the Greeks and Indians
together like this?
Menander will not help.
He will not answer questions put to him.

I must make a child I know so well
crawl to Iphigenia

who still hears voices in dreams:
What is that star that swims across the sky?

Her father speaking,
or is it mine, palms raised under a blue sky.

Some things are not in our power.
Longing for his power to be quick.

Love like a black stone,
whatever that might mean.

What can the poem stay?
A shoreline razed by dark fishing lines

as Iphigenia knelt, head turned to the east,
murmuring: Amma come, come quick!

As if a mother's hands could
thrust the sail back into time's rift,

shield a young throat bared to the wind.
Why did he do that?

What was Agamemnon's rage?
What might have become of Iphigenia
growing older
had she survived?

In seeking answers
the hardest script will do.

A child's upright hand –
stony syntax, slow work

in part-time English,
trying to forge an honest sentence

such as:
Someone has cut her cords.

Or: *Someone will swim farther
and farther from what she feels is the shore.*

INDIAN APRIL

I

Allen Ginsberg on a spring day you stopped
naked in a doorway in Rajasthan.

You were preparing to wash, someone took a snapshot:
I see your left hand bent back
cigarette in your mouth,

metal basin set at your ankles
heat simmering at the edges of your skin
in Indian air, in water.

Rinsed clean you squatted at the threshold again,
struck a bhajan on a tin can.

Watched Mira approach, her hair a black mass
so taut it could knock over a lamppost,
skin on her fists raw from rubbing chipped honeypots.

In the middle distance
like a common bridegroom,
Lord Krishna rides a painted swing.

You ponder this, not sure
if an overdose of poetry
might crash a princess.

Later in the alleyway you note
a zither leapt from a blind baul's fist.

William Blake's death mask,
plaster cast with the insignia of miracles.

In a burning ghat the sensorium's ruin:
a man's spine and head poked with a stick

so bone might crisp into ash, vapors spilled
into terrible light where the Ganga pours.

II

I was born at the Ganga's edge.
My mother wrapped me in a bleached sari,
laid me in stiff reeds, in hard water.

I tried to keep my nostrils above mud,
learnt how to use my limbs, how to float.

This earth is filled with black water,
small islands with bristling vines afford us some hold.

Tired out with your journals you watch
Mira crouch by the rough stones of the alley.
Her feet are bare, they hurt her.

So much flight for a poet, so much persistence.
Allen Ginsberg, where are you now?

55

Engine of flesh, hot sunflower of Mathura,
teach us to glide into life,

teach us when not to flee,
when to rejoice, when to weep,

teach us to clear our throats.

III

Kaddish, Kaddish I hear you cry
in the fields of Central Park.

He brought me into his tent
and his banner over me was love.

I learn from you that the tabernacles of grace
are lodged in the prickly pear,

the tents of heaven torn by sharp vines,
running blackberry,
iron from the hummingbird's claw.

He brought me into his tent
and his banner over me was love.

Yet now he turns his face from me.
Krishna you are my noose, I your knife.

And who shall draw apart
from the misericord of attachment?

IV

Holy the cord of death, the sensual palaces
of our feasting and excrement.

Holy, the waters of the Ganga, Hudson, Nile,
Pamba, Mississippi, Mahanadi.

Holy the lake in Central Park, bruised eye of earth,
mirror of heaven,

where you leap beard first
this April morning, resolute, impenitent,

not minding the pointed reeds, spent syringes,
pale, uncoiled condoms.

You understood the kingdom of the quotidian,
groundhogs in heat, the arrhythmia of desire.

I see you young again
teeth stained with betel and bhang,

nostrils tense with the smoke of Manhattan,
ankles taut in a yogic asana, prickly with desire.

You who sang America are flush now with death,
your poems – bits of your spine and skull –

ablaze in black water drawing you on.
Allen Ginsberg your flesh is indigo,

the color of Krishna's face, Mira's bitter grace.
Into hard water you leap, drawing me on.

I hear you call: *Govinda, aaou, aaou!*

TAXICABWALLAH

Darkling I listen . . .
— *Keats*

I crouched in the back of the taxicab, sleeves sweaty, watched my face quivering in the mirror. *Choli ka piche, dum, dum. Choli ka niche, dum, dum.* Glimpsed his blunt head, kirpan out of sight as he hummed. Shoving back the glass he whispered a name, Paramjit. Right by the Chrysler Building he swerved, struck a roadblock. The headlights in slow unison fell out, one by one. Our yellow-bodied metal thing snorted fire. To sharp sirens, police bullhorns, arc of fierce lights pandering, Paramjit Singh and I became one thing. I stepped out in my new leather skirt, shaking. No sir, we were not running from anything. I watched Paramjit hands up against the wall, handcuffs glittering. You wanted that, I thought. That you wanted.

Later he came to me, through the walls of my bedroom, face bound in a scrap of pink, damp where the eyeholes were. He knelt by my bed. I saw the dead ranged in his head. No pretty sight. Defense Colony, Delhi. He was under the dusty neem tree when the mobs came. His father, an old man, had his throat slit. The tree so clumsy, branches shaking. Smoke in the old man's hair from a cigarette someone set there. Blood in his boots, in the scraps of paper torn from vegetable wrappings. Batala, Ludhiana, Amritsar, where your grandparents grew old, I murmured. And before that, Lahore, the terrible train rides at Partition time. I shut my eyes, feeling his ribs under mine.

I took Paramjit walking by the fountain where a man all dressed in black, a silk turban on his head, was tossing fire-brands. He took one up, plunged it into his mouth. The crowd roared. Paramjit held on to my hand, his bones so light, lime leaves dropping into smoke. Learn to toss fire-brands in the new world, I thought, learn to swallow them. I stood by the edge of the sandpit watching the performer, with sharp lips, sunken eyes, crying out *Fuego! Fuego!* Paramjit crouched down making a shadow. In the tree clumsy with branches, a bird started warbling. Paramjit what is it? Nightingale! He was shaking as he replied. In school in Batala we by–hearted the poem. His voice broke in my ears as traffic throbbed. I reached for his hand. He stumbled with me to West Fourth, the street thick with taxicabs.

ILLITERATE HEART

I

One summer holiday I returned
to the house where I was raised.
Nineteen years old, I crouched
on the damp floor where grandfather's
library used to be, thumbed through
Conrad's *Heart of Darkness*
thinking, Why should they imagine no one else
has such rivers in their lives?

I was Marlowe and Kurtz and still more
a black woman just visible at the shore.
I thought, It's all happened, all happened before.

So it was, I began, unsure of the words
I was to use, still waiting for a ghost
to stop me, crying out:
You think you write poetry! Hey you –

as he sidestepped me dressed neatly
in his kurta and dhoti,
a mahakavi from the temples of
right thought.

Or one in white flannels
unerringly English, lured from Dove Cottage,
transfixed by carousels of blood,
Danton's daring, stumbling over stones
never noticing his outstretched
hand passed through me.

      II

How did I come to this script?
Amma taught me from the Reading Made Easy
books, steps 1 & 2, pointed out Tom and Bess
little English children
sweet vowels of flesh they mouthed to perfection:
aa ee ii oo uu a (apple) b (bat) c (cat) d (dat).
Dat? I could not get, so keen the rhymes made me,
sense overthrown.

Those children wore starched knickerbockers
or sailor suits and caps,
waved Union Jacks,
tilted at sugar beets.

O white as milk
their winding sheets!

I imagined them dead all winter
packed into icicles,
tiny and red, frail homunculus each one
sucking on alphabets.

Amma took great care with the books,
wrapped them in newsprint lest something
should spill, set them on the rosewood sill.
When wild doves perched they shook

droplets from quicksilver wings
onto fading covers.

The books sat between Gandhi's *Experiments
with Truth* and a minute crown of thorns
a visiting bishop brought.

He told us that the people of Jerusalem
spoke many tongues including Arabic, Persian,
Syriac, as in our liturgy, Aramaic too.

Donkeys dragged weights through tiny streets.
Like our buffalos, he laughed.
I had to perform my *Jana Gana Mana* for him
and Wordsworth's daffodil poem –
the latter I turned into a rural terror,
my version of the chartered streets.

III

What beats in my heart? Who can tell?
I cannot tease my writing hand around
that burnt hole of sense, figure out the
quickstep of syllables.

On pages where I read the words of Gandhi
and Marx, saw the light of the Gospels,
the script started to quiver and flick.

Letters grew fins and tails.
Swords sprang from the hips of consonants,
vowels grew ribbed and sharp.
Pages bound into leather
turned the color of ink.

My body flew apart:
wrist, throat, elbow, thigh,
knee where a mole rose,
bony scapula, blunt-cut hair,

then utter stillness as a white sheet
dropped on nostrils and neck.

Black milk of childhood drunk
and drunk again!

I longed to be like Tom and Bess
dead flat on paper.

IV

At noon I burrowed through
Malayalam sounds,
slashes of sense, a floating trail.

Nights I raced into the garden.
Smoke on my tongue, wet earth
from twisted roots of banyan
and arbor-tristis.

What burnt in the mirror
of the great house
became a fierce condiment.
A métier almost:

aa I ii u uu au um aha ka kh
ga gha nga cha chha ja ja nja

njana (my sole self), *njaman* (knowledge),
nunni (gratitude), *ammechi, appechan,*
veliappechan (grandfather).

Uproar of sense, harsh tutelage:
aana (elephant), *amma* (tortoise),
ambjuan (lotus).

A child mouthing words
to flee family.

I will never enter that house, I swore,
I'll never be locked in a cage of script.

And the lotus rose, quietly, quietly,
I committed that to memory,
later added: *ce lieu me plaît*
dominé de flambeaux.

      v

In dreams I was a child babbling
at the gate splitting into two,
three to make herself safe.

Grown women combing black hair
in moonlight by the railroad track,
stuck forever at the accidental edge.

O the body in parts,
bruised buttress of heaven!
she cries,

67

a child in a village church
clambering into embroidered vestments
to sing at midnight a high sweet tune.

Or older now
musing in sunlight
combing a few white strands of hair.

To be able to fail.
To set oneself up
so that failure is also possible.

Yes,
that too
however it is grasped.

The movement toward self definition.
A woman walking the streets,
a woman combing her hair.

Can this make music in your head?
Can you whistle hot tunes
to educate the barbarians?

These lines took decades to etch free,
the heart's illiterate,
the map is torn.

Someone I learn to recognize,
cries out at Kurtz, thrusts skulls aside,
lets the floodwaters pour.

For Adrienne Rich

68

RITES OF SENSE

In twilight as she lies on a mat
I rub my mother's feet with jasmine oil,
touch calluses under skin,
joints upholding that fraught original thing –
bone, gristle, skin, all that makes her mine.
All day she swabbed urine from the floor,
father's legs so weak he clung to the rosewood bed.
She rinsed soiled cloths, hung them out to dry
on a coir rope by a vine, its passion fruit
clumsy with age, dangling.

She lies on a mat, a poor thing beached,
belly slack, soles crossed, sari damp and white.
I kneel in darkness at her side,
her oldest child returned for a few weeks
at summer's height.
She murmurs my name,
asks in Malayalam *Why is light so hot?*

Beyond her spine I catch a candle glisten.
The door's a frame for something
I'm too scared to name:
a child, against a white wall,

hands jammed to her teeth, lips torn,
breath staggering its hoarse silence.

All night my voice laced through dreams
tiny eyelets for the smoke,
Amma, I am burning!
I'm a voice slit from sound,
just snitches of blood, loopholes of sweat,
a sack of flesh you shut me in.

What words of passage to that unlit place?
What rites of sense?

Amma, I am dreaming myself into your body.
It is the end of everything.
Your pillow stained with white
tosses as a wave might
on our southern shore.

Will you lay your cheek against mine?
Bless my bent head?

You washed me once, gave me suck,
made me live in your father's house,
taught me to wake at dawn,
sweep the threshold clean of blood-red leaves.
Showed me a patch of earth dug with your hands
where sweet beans grow coiled and raw.

Taught me to fire a copper pan,
starch and fold a sari, raise a rusty needle,

stitch my woman's breath
into the mute amazement of sentences.

72

RED PARAPET

Sister, you live in a very private place
an extremity of sense.

I watch you in mother's garden.
Plucking jasmine petals you set them
in your palm and how they burn.

A rat indigo with rain races
under the banyan tree,
you point it out, prise stones

from soil, lift up your sleeve,
make me see the bruise, blackish,
saffron edged where you hurt yourself.

Touching you I think: We pay with our lives,
they become us,

and I need to write as if penitence were
the province of poems.

Dear sister I pray a time will come
when voices that poke you
with white–hot pincers flicker and drop

harmless as bats in the jamun tree
and monsoon rivers swarm back into clouds,
and waft through the mirror in our grandfather's room,

and time turns tail
in a great unhappening of things,

a cobra
that pours over threshold stones –
I six, you barely one, face shining in my skirts,

gazing as it leapt
clean out of its skin, up the red parapet,
and we smelled ebony flesh,

the whole darting heat of him,
the blessing.

CHENNAI AFTERNOON

Flinty hot, two stones could have raised a fire. Three of us, Anandi, the little one, and I, worked our way across a gravel path to a tongue of rock spat out by the sea. My chappals off, I hitched my sari to my knees. The little one was straining at my thighs, I gripped her tight, pointed out a speck streaming on the horizon: *Noke! Noke!* She bit me like a wildcat might, leaving tooth marks, yelling from that sweet dark throat: I'm going amma into the blue never coming back to you! The seawind hit me tight, I was a ja-mun splashed on rock no breath, no fight. Anandi rushed out, sari dripping salt, grabbed my child who had water streaming from her eyes, so black and beautiful. That night they called from Tiruvella, appa had been ill, heart stopped. The doctors struck him in his ribs, pounded his chest till it hummed again, that slow sad breath which keeps one afloat. It's election time, amma said, just stay home. There are bombs in Chennai. Just last week in the marketplace by the grape stall, a few feet from her mother, a child was blown up, a scrap of her pink frock, all that was left. Why must they scare me so? Is it love that makes fear start? As I thrust the little one apart something burst in me, slow and terrible like the sea.

LOW HILLS OF BAVARIA

The streets of Erlangen are very still,
there is water at the edge of the rooftops.
And in the low hills of Bavaria,
a distinct fragrance
of thyme and wild blackberry.

What is buried here? I ask myself.
What rumor of iron?
What child trapped in ash?

Not far from Nuremberg and its *Tribune*
I stand at the brink of winter to search myself out.
Where can I go? Neither archduchess
in a framed portrait, nor art student,
black portfolio dangling at her hips.

My silks are creased, my hands are empty.
I have left my sack of words behind,
those bruised and jagged syllables.
I have come in search of trees that smolder
when there is very little wind,

dry roots stoking light,
voices that mouth their Sunday hymns

so soundlessly:
O Lamb of God have mercy upon us!
Whose mercy will fall, as the rain falls?

Where are those burning books?
Those *Yarzeit* candles?
Where is that child,
her skin slippery with gas?
Past shelves of gneiss below my path,
lichen scrawled, gray–gold for forgetfulness,
I approach a river dark with ash.

GIVING NAMES TO STONES

Was it the silence in his head that touched you so?
Or the need to know watermelon plots
from his childhood, radishes blunt with color,

haiku composed in the school yard,
seventeen syllables, no more,
yearning's economy,

imitating the Japanese masters,
making up lost time
which is what he brought you,

lips wet with split melon,
hair rushing black water.
Dreams of his grandmother made him mute,

she squatted in the yard of Poston internment camp
picking out stones: *Yoko, Noriko, Miko!*
A fifteen–year–old girl losing her hold, imagine that.

As he held out his hands, pleading,
though what he needed who could tell,
her loneliness lit up in you,

a grown girl giving names to stones.
Ribs mounting under skin so frail,
butterflies could have bored through.

DAFFODILS

Kasuya Eiichi, poet of Japan,
knows a place where daffodils bloom,
a damp place, where hair cut
from heads of young girls
sharpens the wind,
where a moon soars over a cliff
and syllables of speech
melt into petals – ocher petals.

I will ask him to take me there
into that swamp of dreams.
When underground water seeps into my wrists
I'll cry out through the mists:

Come, I'll not flash
daffodil flesh at you. I am older,
I have two children now,
my breasts are jugs of blood,
my hair black with silver

running through makes a pillow for my man,
his thighs cut from river mud,
belly gold with longing.

ROADSIDE MUSIC

I do not know for the life of me
how to sit quietly.
Something takes hold of my feet and makes them fret.

Dust scribbles the way to my mother's house.
When I shut my eyes, all that red dust
makes my room disappear.

How should I sit still, how should I write poems?
I find a chair and set it by the window.
The leaves are very dark, filled with water.

In all this solitude the wind in the leaves
makes a sound like skinned onions
rolling off the kitchen counter.

She comes to me, Ono no Komachi,
in a kimono of pale silk.
She leans against a stone at the side of the road.

Out of her ribs come the cries of a lover
she forced into the cold:
Ono, why Ono?

Her hair shakes free of its pins,
her kimono bursts.
This too enters her poems.

Someday shall I wait as she did,
quietly scoring lines into roadside music?
Will this desk disappear and closet and kitchen?

How sharp the reeds at the river's brink.
I am lonely she writes, *like a reed root-cut.*
If the river called, she'd go, I think.

WATER TABLE

A river flows under my window,
on its surface, I'll set a table.
Legs underwater, the tabletop rocks,
birds flock to watch:

I lay a basket of eggs on the table,
speckled rounds, polished with silk,
I set a bowl of milk,
two mangoes freckled pink.

I set sleep on that table, dreams,
and all the yearning that ever welled up,
streaked with indigo from the fields
of Champaran, long-grained rice,
roots blue as steel.

Under the shadow of my hands
the table shifts on heavy water.
I cry to those I love:
I have set a table for you,
come, come, quick!

POEM IN LATE OCTOBER

I watch you – hair ruffled, shirt tucked in
over the thing that is making you ill.
You let yourself into the yellow cab
after me, gingerly, whispering:
I love this light, October's real isn't it?
You tug your book bag
after you delicately as a pregnant woman might.

Now what is real casts a shadow
that blues itself against the body's mass –
ribs, liver, pancreas,
the mad zone of cells, swelling.

On the road to St. Vincent's Hospital
the trees are thick with sap.
There is mist in the restaurants
where we used to lunch,
piecing together oddments of our lives.

The notes on Trollope you penned
for an encyclopedia;
the book I dream of writing
set in the transit lounges of my childhood;
Your unfinished memoir; chair, rug, candle

in your living room
lit by ordinary lamplight
and down below the fitful traffic on Jane Street.

I imagine you now in that other city
magnificent, cast out of the entrails of this
in a sky that does not waver with autumn light.
Late pansies burn in window boxes.
Under the blue canopy of the hospital
other hands take you in and I cannot follow.

Hard, hard, this going under
the etch of the legible where we domicile ourselves
as light draws us out and we enter late October.

There is nothing in my hands
and you must walk through water.

In memory of Walter Kendrick, 1947–98

DIARY OF DREAMS

Before my birth
a republic was dreamt
fought for with prayers,
burnt indigo, and steel.

At the edge of a waterwheel
soldiers stumble,
the scent of guava
clings to their heels.

A child in white
points to a house,
the threshold bloody:
Is this all too simple?

I love you Gandhiji,
the child cries out,
I want to be a satyagrahi!
Down the stone steps

strides Gandhiji,
his charka glints,
he is pale and thin,
under his breath

he calls to the girl:
Here, come
make salt with me!
She knows

he is her grandfather,
she lifts up her petticoat,
she skips to him.
But the guava tree is raw,

the gatepost crumbles,
out of pocked wood red ants crawl.
The steps of the house
make a breaking wave.

In Pokharan's desert
a bright bomb
caves soil
into feverish ruins.

The wind is slow
torn leaves variable.
Truth has a deeper hold
than perishing.

On getting the order
the house must be burnt,
the soldiers wipe boots,
gather fuel.

They do not know
what a pilgrimage means.
Why a woman kneels
in a floating room,

gashed remembrance,
a green orchard burning.
These are my syllables
of clear water,

small scale jottings
from a new republic.
Diary of dreams,
drawer of ransacked silk.

Heart's hope,
grief's consonant.
Salt fumes
in a red desert.

BLACK RIVER, WALLED GARDEN

I

The garden of my childhood flees from me:
scent of cloves at the point of decay,
citadel of orchids swollen with rain,

runnels of black earth
where rosebushes sprang clotted with mist
and on small rocks, sharp stars of jasmine and saughandi,

milkwhite seasons of longing,
serendipitous under the first gate
where the kingfisher taps its beak against wood:

Tat-tat-tat!
That-that-that!
Tat tvam asi!

II

At six, hidden by the gooseberry bush,
its spiky leaves a halo for my face,
Look I'm an angel!

I cried to cousin Koshi
who scuffed up dirt
with his heels, lit up a stolen beedi,

made out he didn't care:
Don't touch my canoe –
see if you dare!

The river's in spate.
It bears my face away.
The canoe hangs from a jackfruit tree,

dark spoke under succulent thorns,
hull afloat with spider threads,
eggs of the copper-colored beetle,
delicate fibers of the nesting butterfly.

III

Last night in my bed in Peterborough
under a cherry-colored blanket
in midsummer as the moon beat down

on rough meadow grass,
the call of the hermit thrush in my ears,
I dreamt that childhood river:

black waters cutting and clashing,
wrists slit by raw sugarcane stalks,
a child crying to Jesus.

And how she fell:
ring after ring into the well,
the sore snare of it,

92

green ferns at the rim
slaking the bruise.
About her anklebone, a rope.

IV

→ Ophelia: Sings while collecting flowers (handwritten annotation)

Hurt makes us sing – a sweet foreboding.
Jacob and his angel, a muscular craze, one might say,
the ladder dismantled.

The two of them caught in a daze,
a summer's fever.

I will call this place Peniel.
Under the roaring blue
I come to you perpetually.

Whose words? Whose promise?
Am I a ghost, an aspect of an angel?
Who will bring him back to answer to me?

V

Now was that where I meant to go?
Or was I waylaid?
Call it anamnesis, living memory,

torchlit flesh.
At epiphany
the earliest Christians gathered

and over their heads
shot tongues of flame.
Raised by a fire altar,

93

you understand these things:
the need for human ritual,
plenitude of silence.

But also disorder of speech,
lives where drums beat
anarchic, implosive.

VI

I am a field of wild flowers
stitched without fortune,
grandmother wrote during her travels in China,

forty–seven years old, my age,
three years from her end.

She sent back photos of herself in pale silk
next to the Great Wall, her friend Miss Hartley by her,
the two of them clasping a Bible.

What I miss about home
is the simplicity of our church services
and my little daughter combing out her curls.

[handwritten annotation: Grandmother's words]

Mother saved that letter
with its neat stepping scrawl.

[handwritten annotation: describing handwriting]

[handwritten annotation: reflection: looking back]

VII

Did grandmother go into the room of books ever?
No, it was your grandfather's, hers was the rosewood
room, the one with the mirror you stared in.

[handwritten annotation: bed, Seperate rooms divorce]

94

You seemed in such a daze,
backward running from the library,
slit your ankle at the bone against my mother's rice-pattern cup,

the one she brought home from Shanghai.
You were twirling it on your thumb.
You needed seven stitches, remember?

accident;
— daughter
slit ankle

We had to get a basin for the blood,
one would have thought all the drains
in Mohenjo Daro were flowing!

VIII

→ Grandfather; had
affairs; in library

Who could I tell about the library?
What grandfather did with fingers, lips, thighs,
within sight of Bibles, encyclopedias, dictionaries.

O books with seeing eyes!
I blacked it all away.

→ books; eyes;
could give evidence

In the walled garden on hot mornings
I ditched ants from the love-apple tree
onto my belly and thighs,

lay still as they pinched and struck.
Afternoons I gazed into well water
watching a balloon child,

a Nowhere–Girl, her flesh striking
stone rings as she fell,
face tucked into a metal bucket.

95

Somewhere a mirror smashed.
Ten thousand bits of glass
pierced my sight.

I drank sugar grains mixed with acid,
my hair stood on end.
Burning–Hair–Girl I called myself

] puberty

just as I was sprouting it everywhere –
under my arms, between my thighs,
and my nipples grew large and brown as lakes.

At ten I swung in a tree, skin itching
as cinnamon clouds skimmed the blue.
At eleven I paged through the book grandfather gave me,

pausing at Anna with her honey–colored hair,
the glint of metal in the railroad track
making her heart pucker and start,

Anna Karenina (2.)

till at the very end she fell –
a sentence of blood I could not spell.
Rain dimmed my eyes as I lay in the tree.

I felt the great storm lashing me.
My muslin dress crushed with hail
that pounded down –

a comfort after the shame of so much wet.
I shut my eyes, slid down,
down, into the merciful trunk of the tree.

x *Grandfather's death*

That April of my life
when everything slowed down for me
I saw clouds drift

through the mirror in the rosewood room.
Grandmother's eyes in the portrait
made in her thirtieth year

started to smoke, lost coals,
when a fire is fanned.
Grandfather lay dying in his wooden bed.

They forced morphine into his veins
so he wouldn't bite
and tear the covering sheet to bits.

An old man's skin
hung on the bathroom hook
moldy and flecked with rain.

The mint bush in the garden had tiny stains,
love-apple leaves, rust holes.
His sweat seeped through the foundation stones.

I lay in a grave I dug in the earth.
I swayed in a cradle hung in a tree
and all of the visible world –

walled garden,
black river – flowed in me.

XI

Must I stoop,
drink from those waters again,
reach a walled garden, memory's unquiet place?

Will I see a child under a tree?
Was she the one the poet traveler sought,
the sunspot in her thigh so hot

he was forced to cry
Prajnaparamita, burn with me!
Till the Indian Ocean and the salt waters of the Atlantic

rocked him free, the arms of the girl
a bent ship of longing,
her hair the skin of a muddied garden,

Grandfather's affair

feverish source of ruin, as
over the anthills, leaves swirl
in an alphabet no tongue can replicate.

I see her as she skips to the garden gate.
What burns in me now
is the black coal of her face.

secretive, escaping

Shall I turn, make peace,
peace to the first gate
she will never enter again?

XII

The leaves of the rose tree
splinter and flee; the garden
of my childhood returns to the sea.

98

The piecework of sanity,
the fretwork of desire,
restive bits and pieces edged into place,

satisfies so little.
In dreams come calling
migrant missing selves,

fire in an old man's sleeve,
coiled rosebuds struck from a branch.
Our earthly world slit open.

NOTES

"Elegy for My Father"
As I finish this poem, a warm rain falls. There is lightening in
the air. The makings of a storm. My father loved storms. He
called them "nature's glory." I began this poem in New York
City, and now exactly a year after his death I am in Pandan
Valley, Singapore. *Almav* is Malayalam for soul. *Almav avide*
means roughly "There's the soul!"

"Reading Rumi As the Phone Rings"
While I have freely invented what I imagine to be Shams ul
Din's words, for the lines from Rumi's poetry I am deeply in-
debted to separate translations from the Persian by A. J. Ar-
berry and Coleman Barks.

"Muse" to "Valley" poem cycle
In this cycle of poems, I have tried to catch something of the
internal architecture of sense, the objects of our metamorphic
life – a trajectory from the pitch of memory to the possibility of
a shared existence. Yet I am haunted by what my words can
barely mark, what for want of a better term I invoke as *muse*,
that invisible space where meaning is made and unmade.

"Muse"
Malayalam, my mother tongue, is the language of Kerala, on
the southwest coast of India.

"Choric Meditation"
When Grand Central Station in New York City was being re-
modeled, there was a pasteboard I had to pass on my way to
work. It had large pictures of Maurice Sendak's Wild Things,
from his picture book for children.

"Map"
The lines in italic are from my poem "Indian Sandstone" (*River and Bridge: Poems*, 1996).

"Civil Strife"
The tale of the girl who turned into a flowering tree was much in my mind. I am indebted to the lovely translation by the poet A. K. Ramanujan in his book *Folktales from India* (1991).

"Indigo"
Ai is the Japanese word for indigo. I was inspired by the work of the artist Hiroyuki Shindo. In parts of India, peasants were forced to grow indigo by the British colonizers.

"Gold Horizon"
The lines "*Kya, kya . . .*" and "*Namal ivide . . .*" are renderings in colloquial Hindi and Malayalam, respectively, of the questions "Who are we here?" and "What are we here?"

"Indian April"
This poem was composed in memory of Allen Ginsberg. In the third part of the poem the words "He brought me into his tent . . ." come from the Song of Solomon in the Bible; "Krishna you are my noose . . ." comes from a rough rendering of Mirabai's lines.

"Illiterate Heart"
"And the lotus rose, quietly, quietly" is from T. S. Eliot's *Four Quartets*; "*ce lieu me plaît / dominé de flambeaux*" is from Paul Valèry's *Cimetière Marin*. As part of my early studies, I had to learn a portion of each poem by heart.

"Daffodils"
This poem was inspired by Kasuya Eiichi's poem "Daffodils," but also running through my head was that other poem, William Wordsworth's "I Wandered Lonely as a Cloud," which I read as a child in India without ever having glimpsed these yellow-gold trumpets.

"Roadside Music"
Ono no Komachi was woman poet of ninth-century Japan.
The tale of her wandering and possession appear in the Noh
play *Sotoba Komachi* by Kwanami.

"Black River, Walled Garden"
The poet traveler is Octavio Paz, and I was inspired by his
poem *"Cuento de Dos Jardines."* I first read it in the garden of my
childhood in Tiruvella, India. Paz speaks of his childhood gar-
den in Mixcoac, Mexico: *"Aquel de Mixcoac, abandonado, / cubierto
de cicatrices, / era un cuerpo / a punto de desplomarse."* In section 5, the
"you" who is addressed is my friend Roshni Rustomji-Kerns.

ACKNOWLEDGMENTS

My gratitude to Reg Gibbons for his belief in my poetry and his care and encouragement of this book. Okwui Enwezor for inviting me to compose "Notebook." Vijay Seshadri for helping me arrange the manuscript according to the music of the poems.

My thanks to those who helped me live my life as I wrote these poems. Gauri Viswanathan, dear friend and sister soul. Verghis Koshi, my cousin who keeps me in earshot of child-hood. Erika Duncan who helps me keep faith with the writing life. Walter Kendrick who shared chitchat and dream talk till the end.

David Lelyveld, whose love sustains. Adam Kuruvilla and Svati Mariam who bring me joy. My mother and my sisters Anna and Elsa across the dark waters, in India. My father in whose memory I have made this book, who taught me to hope that lines scribbled in a secret notebook might one day enter the world.

I am grateful to the MacDowell Colony for a time of great quiet and concentration that allowed me to compose several of these poems. The National University of Singapore for a season as poet in residence. The New York Foundation for the Arts for a Poetry Fellowship.

I am grateful to the following publications in which these po-ems first appeared:

Ariel: "Illiterate Heart," "She Hears a Gold Flute"
Brooklyn Review: "Reading Rumi As the Phone Rings"
Café Review: "Chennai Afternoon"
Chandrabhaga: "Diary of Dreams"
Chelsea: "Water Table"

Crab Orchard Review: "An Honest Sentence," "Taxicabwallah"

Feminist Studies: "Rites of Sense," "Port Sudan." Reprinted with permission.

Hybridity: Journal of Cultures, Texts and Identities: "Elegy for My Father"

Journal of Literature and Aesthetics: "Valley"

Kavya Bharati: "Chennai Afternoon"

Massachusetts Review special issue, *A Tribute to Allen Ginsberg and American Poetry:* "Indian April"

Performing Hybridity (University of Minnesota Press, 1999): "Man in a Red Shirt"

Persimmon: Asian Literature, Arts, and Culture: "Map"

Seneca Review: "Heat Wave"

Toronto Review of Contemporary Writing Abroad: "Black River, Walled Garden"

Weber Studies special issue, *Indian American Literature:* "Fragments," "Daffodils," "Gold Horizon"

Women's Review of Books: "Low Hills of Bavaria," "Red Parapet"

The World: "Translated Lives"

Under the title of "Notebook" a cycle of poems ("Muse," "Choric Meditation," "Provenance," "Fragments," "Map," "House," "Civil Strife," "Indigo," "Mirror of Earth," "Glyphs," "Valley," "Translated Lives," and "Man in a Red Shirt") was published as part of the catalog for *The Mirror's Edge*, at the Bildmuseet, Umea, Sweden, 1999. "Notebook" appeared in an English text with Swedish translations.